Introduction

The aim of this book is to provide resources to help busy Key Stage 1 teachers introduce practical science activities into their National Curriculum and QCA science lessons. The book covers the topics:
• Sound & Hearing
• Forces and Motion
The book provides a series of lessons with a number of different practical activities on the same theme. Individual classroom teachers will wish to choose which activities are most appropriate for their own individual situation. Each lesson has detailed notes for teachers giving learning objectives for each activity. Assessment activities can be found at the end of each section in the book.

Topical Resources
P.O. Box 329
Broughton
Preston
Lancashire
PR3 5LT

Topical Resources publishes a range of Educational Materials for use in Primary Schools and Pre-School Nurseries and Playgroups.

For the latest catalogue:
Tel: 01772 863158
Fax: 01772 866153
e.mail: sales@topical-resources.co.uk
Buy online at:
www.topical-resources.co.uk

Copyright © 2007 Viki Mason
Illustrated by: 'Art Works'
69 Worden Lane, Leyland
Designed by Paul Sealey Design Services, 3 Wentworth Drive, Thornton, Lancashire.
Printed in the UK for 'Topical Resources' by T.Snape and Co Ltd, Boltons Court, Lancashire.

First published September 2007
ISBN 978 1 905509 55 3

GW01564113

Contents

This book has been written for Key Stage One teachers to use in Science lessons. The activities have been carried out successfully with Year 1 and Year 2 pupils in different schools. The objectives covered follow the QCA requirements for Science at Key Stage One, but can still be used if your school does not follow the QCA guidelines.

The thinking behind this publication stems from a knowledge of different learning styles. All our pupils learn in different ways and this book aims to enable the Key Stage One teacher to cater for all types of learner. Whether our pupils are visual, auditory or kinaesthetic learners we must remember their needs above our own. Visual teachers tend to teach in a predominantly visual way which discourages other pupils from accessing the information as well as they could do. Our pupils need to be encouraged to join in activities which stimulate them and excite them. They need to be encouraged to speak and listen well while working together in a group. The collaborative carousel approach to learning is particularly successful with Key Stage One classes. The pupils encounter many different short tasks within one Science session where they can be involved in discussion, cutting/ sticking activities, role play, 'hands-on' tasks, active listening, sharing resources, working together, taking turns and carrying out investigations.

Teacher Notes

Although these lesson activities are presented in a carousel style approach, the teacher may decide to work through the tasks as whole class sessions, concentrating on one task at a time. Alternatively, the tasks can be managed by a classroom support assistant working with small groups outside the allocated Science lesson times if required.

Carousel Approach

The class will be organised into small mixed ability groups of approximately five or six pupils for each task. Using timers, the pupils take turns to carry out each task, and then move on to the next activity. The timer you use depends on how long you have for your Science lesson. It could be anything from a 10 minute to a 20 minute timer.

The Benefits of Working Collaboratively

Collaborative working enables the children to:

- Co-operate in a group situation.
- Take turns.
- Share resources.
- Listen carefully to each other.
- Develop their thinking skills.
- Take on roles within the group - leader, scribe, reader etc.
- Work with other pupils of mixed ability.
- Work with pupils outside their 'friendship group'.
- Complete work within a given period of time.
- Carry out 'challenges' which they wouldn't normally be able to do.
- Become independent learners.

Sound and Hearing

Main Objective:
To understand that there are many different sources of sound

Talk about:
Have a selection of instruments at the front of the classroom. Play some of these and ask the children to close their eyes to listen to each sound. Then ask them to open their eyes and listen to the sounds they can hear around them in school. Ask questions such as "What can you tell me about sounds?" Encourage them to share ideas with a partner before they share them with the class. Keep the questions open-ended to find out what the children already know about this topic. Next play some of the instruments again but ask the children to put their hands over their ears and then remove them. They can keep doing this while you play. Then ask what they can you tell you about how we hear sound? Explain that they are going to find out much more about sound by carrying out some exciting tasks.

Activity 1: Play the 'Sounds Quiz'
Objective: To identify and compare the sounds made by different musical instruments.
Resources: Various musical instruments as identified on Activity Sheet 1, a curtain or cloth to hold up as a screen.
Task: Support or ask two children to hold the curtain. Hide the instruments behind the cloth. A volunteer child or adult helper should play each instrument one at a time. Group members should put up a hand and suggest what instrument made the sound. Record how many guesses are needed before the correct instrument is chosen and then write the instrument's name. Finally, decide if this instrument made a loud or quiet noise. If time, another child can play the instruments in a different order.

Activity 2: How do musical instruments make sounds?
(adult help required)
Objective: To understand that we can make sounds in a variety of ways.
Resources: A stringed instrument, a drum, a recorder and a tambourine. Several plastic tubs, several elastic bands, pencils, plastic bottles, cardboard boxes, rice, small stones, straws, lolly sticks etc.
Task: Place a selection of musical instruments on the table. Let the children take turns to play an instrument and talk about how the sound is made. Help them to identify where the sound comes from. Look at the moving parts and where the air moves through the instrument. Next ask children to make their own sound maker from the junk materials provided. Encourage plenty of conversation about sounds while they are choosing and making. Ask questions such as "Why are you choosing those? What could make a louder/ quieter sound? How will you play it? How will you fix it together? Tell me a good name for your sound maker" etc. Finally, fill in the worksheet showing what you did to make different sounds.

Activity 3: How can you stop sound getting into your ears?
(adult help required)
Objective: To understand that we hear with our ears.
Resources: Different ear protectors as shown on the sheet, headphones, earphones, ear muffs and rubber ear defenders; musical instruments as shown on the sheet.
Task: There are health and safety considerations here. The children need to know that it is dangerous to put objects into their ears. The rubber ear defenders must be cleaned with an antiseptic wipe before each use. Children should be warned that loud noises including loud music can actually damage the ear. Ask the group to take turns to wear the ear protectors while the teacher makes the different sounds each time. Children should record their results on the worksheet.

Activity 4: What different sounds can you hear on a listening walk?
(adult help required)
Objectives: To make observations of sounds by listening carefully. To explore sounds using their sense of hearing.
Resources: Clipboards and pencils for the group, Activity Sheet 4 for each child.
Task: Walk around the classroom or school listening for any sounds. Children record ideas in their own way on the sheet provided. As they walk ask questions such as "What can you hear? Where is it coming from? How can you tell? Which sound is louder? Which sound is softer? Which part of the room/school is the quietest at the moment?" At the end of the walk record the loudest sounds and the quietest sounds.

Plenary
Ask the class to tell you one thing they have found out about sound. They could tell their partners first, then share ideas with the class. This will encourage those less able to participate with the discussion. Encourage them to discuss the many different sounds heard and the different ways sounds can be made. Finally, talk about how sound travels through the air and enters our ears.

Play the 'Sounds Quiz'

Name: _____ Date: _____

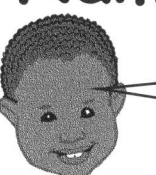

Play an instrument behind a curtain. How many guesses until your friend / group know what it is? Is it a loud or quiet sound?

| bell | chime bar | rain stick | triangle | wood block |
| tambourine | hand clap | shout | xylophone | drum |

Tally of guesses (e.g. ⟋⟋⟋⟋)	Name of Instrument	Was it loud or quiet? Circle the correct word.	
		loud	quiet
		loud	quiet
		loud	quiet
		loud	quiet
		loud	quiet
		loud	quiet
		loud	quiet
		loud	quiet
		loud	quiet
		loud	quiet

How do Musical Instruments Make Sounds?

Name: Date:

Try to make a sound with these objects. Write/draw what you did.

Musical Instrument	What you did to make a sound	Musical Instrument	What you did to make a sound
guitar		recorder	
drum		tambourine	

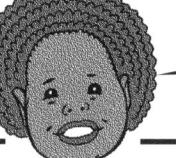

Use junk materials to make your own musical instrument. Draw it below.

My own musical instrument	How I made a sound

How many different ways did you make a sound?

How Can You Stop Sound Getting into Your Ears?

Name: _____   Date: _____

Try these ways of stopping sound. Which works best? Tick the box if you can hear the sound.

Ways of Stopping Sound					
Stereo Headphones					
Furry Ear Muffs					
Workmen's Ear Defenders					
Hands over Ears					

Which stopped the most sound?

Why was this best?

What different sounds can you hear on a 'Listening Walk'?

Name: _____   Date: _____

Go on a listening walk around your school.
Stay **very quiet** and note in each box what you hear.

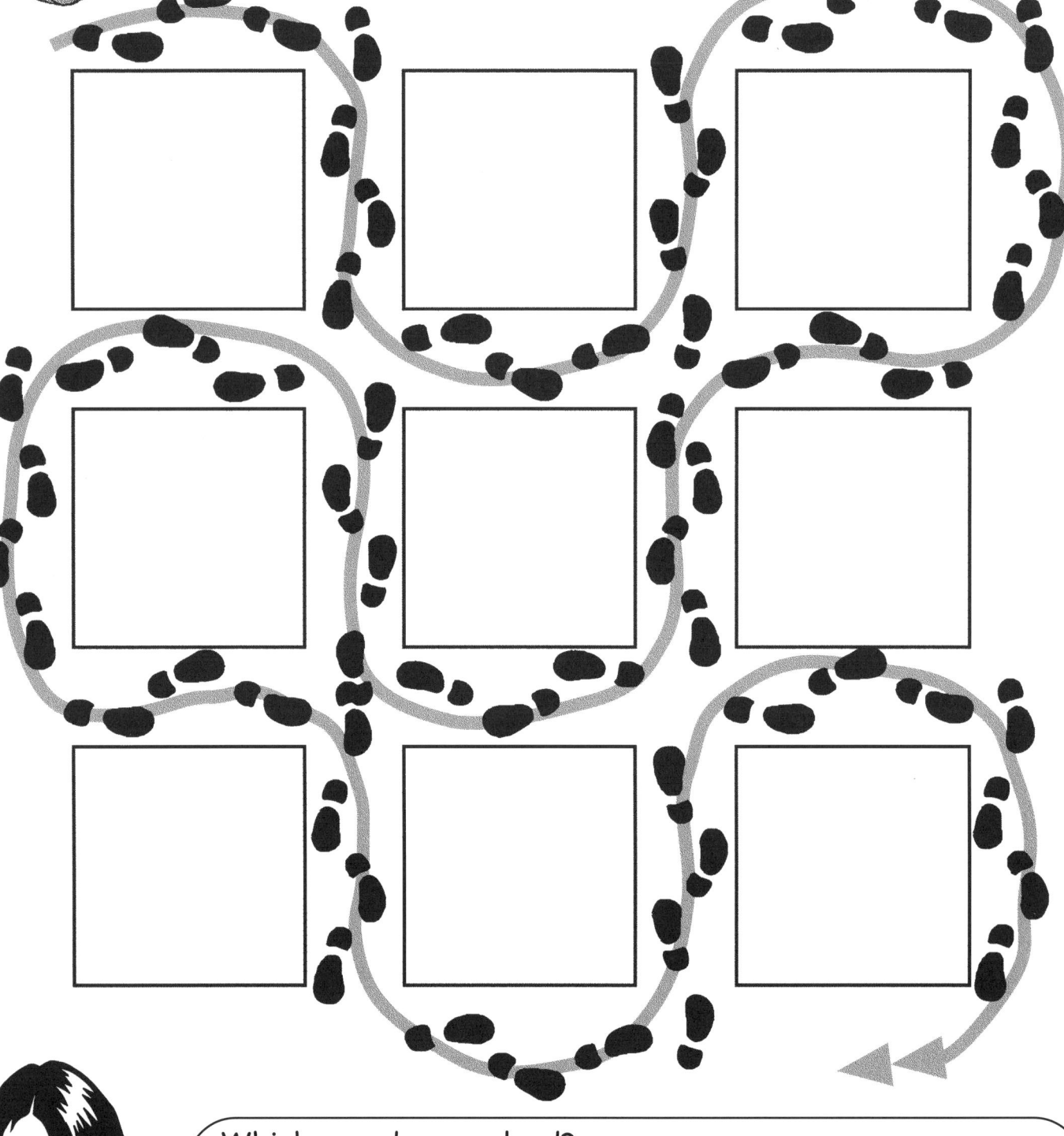

Which sounds were loud?

_____

Which sounds were quiet?

_____

Main Objective:
To understand that sound varies according to distance from the source.
To understand that different objects make different sounds.

Talk about:
Show photos/pictures of various 'noise makers' e.g. thunder, ambulance siren, police siren, aeroplane, tumble drier, ticking clock, drum etc. Ask the children to think of some other 'noise makers' at home and then at school. Write up a list on the board. In pairs ask the children to think of things, which make quiet / loud sounds. Share with the class. Ask a child to come to the front and repeatedly clap their hands. At the same time ask another child to tiptoe away from the sound slowly, right to the edge of the classroom. Ask them to talk about what happened.

Activity 1: Sounds a long way away
(adult help required)
Objective: To understand that sounds seem louder the nearer you are to the source. To measure distances using non-standard or standard measures.
Resources: A ticking clock, an alarm clock, radio and a CD player. Tape measure, ruler, beanbags.
Task: Tell the group to stand in a circle facing outwards around the ticking clock holding a bean bag. Listen to the ticking and then walk away from it slowly. Drop the beanbag on the ground when they can no longer hear the sound. The children take turns to measure the distance walked and record the results on the worksheet. Talk about any differences they have noticed. Repeat the task with different sound sources and talk about what happened. Finally, ask each child to record what happens when you walk away from sounds.

Activity 2: How do musical instruments make sounds?
Objective: To understand that we can make sounds in a variety of ways.
Resources: Several different musical instruments on the table which can be plucked, hit, shaken or blown through; coloured pencils.
Task: Place selection of musical instruments on the table for the group to examine. Let them experiment with plucking, hitting, shaking and blowing to make sounds. Draw an instrument in each box on their work sheet. Use a coloured pencil to show where each instrument moves or has air moving through it. Finally choose one instrument to sketch in more detail with labels showing the moving parts.

Activity 3: How loud is that sound?
Objective: To consider whether a sound is quiet or loud.
Resources: Photos/ pictures showing various 'noise makers' (see worksheet).
Task: Cut out the pictures at the bottom of the worksheet and arrange them along the 'Sound Line' from the quietest to the loudest. Share with a friend before sticking the pictures down. Finally collect magazine pictures /draw your own showing other sound sources. Arrange and glue these along the line in appropriate places.

Activity 4: True or False?
Objective: To describe sounds using a range of appropriate vocabulary.
Resources: Activity Sheet 4 and some true/ false cards – rectangle of card with 'True' written on one side and 'False' written on the other.
Task: As a group answer the questions on the 'True or False' test. A group member/ adult could read out the question and the children show their card, either 'true side up' or 'false side up' to answer. Record the group vote to each question by putting ticks in the appropriate boxes. At the end of the test discuss each question in turn with the teacher in the plenary session.

Plenary
Talk about the activities the children have taken part in and the different sounds encountered. Ask questions such as "How did sounds vary when you moved away from them? How do musical instruments make sounds? What do you do to instruments to make them work? Are some sounds louder than others? Finally, discuss all of the statements in the 'True or False' test and discover which group did best.

Sounds a Long Way Away

Name: _____ Date: _____

Walk away from things that make a sound. Drop a bean-bag when you cannot hear the sound and measure the distance walked.

Sound Made by...	Distance Walked
Ticking Clock	
Alarm Clock	
CD Player	
Radio	

What happens when you walk away from sounds?

_____

How do Musical Instruments Make Sounds?

Name: _____   **Date:** _____

Draw pictures to show how you play some instruments. Choose from the instruments on your table.

This is a _____	This is a _____
This is a _____	This is a _____
This is a _____	This is a _____

Use a coloured pencil to show where the instrument moves or where the air comes out to make a sound.

How Loud is that Sound?

Name: _____ **Date:** _____

Cut out the pictures. Talk about how loud each one is. Stick them on the sound scale.

Quiet

Loud

Now add some sounds of your own. Are they noisy or quiet?

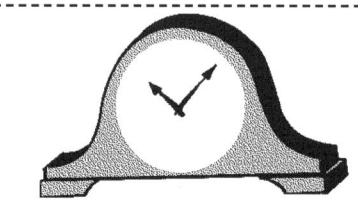

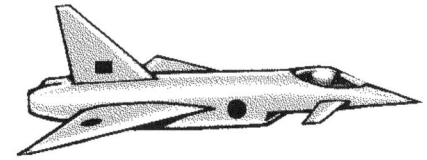

True or False?

Name: _____   **Date:** _____

Take turns to read each statement and then put a tick in either the true or false box.

Statements	True	False
Sounds are made by air moving through or over objects.		
A drum makes a louder sound than a triangle.		
A person talking is quieter than a person whispering.		
Ear muffs help us to hear more clearly.		
If you stand nearer to a sound it will be louder.		
There are no sounds in the whole school today.		
A bell makes a loud sound.		
A sound will get quieter when you move away from it.		

Can you make a sound by using two pieces of card?

Main Objective:
To make predictions, observations, simple comparisons and explain these.

Talk about:
Display different musical instruments and cards with labels at the front of the class. The labels include words such as: shake, pluck, hit and blow. The children can take turns to match the cards to the instruments. Ask the children to mime how each instrument is played. Show them a number scale from 0 to 10, 10 being the loudest sound and 0 being no sound. Ask them to show using their fingers, whiteboards or number fans where each instrument would be on our sound scale. Play each one and decide on scores to mark on the board.

Activity 1: Plan and carry out a listening investigation.
(adult help required)
Objective: To understand that sounds can be made in many different ways. To recognise that when they make sounds something moves/ vibrates.
Resources: Straws, scissors, Sellotape.
Task: As a group plan the investigation by discussing the headings of the boxes found on the planning sheets. (N.B. The first planning sheet is harder than the second one.) The children must ensure that they play the straw whistles in exactly the same way each time for the test to be fair. Repeat the task with straws of varying length, width and shape. Talk about any differences in sound they have noticed. Record the investigation in pictures with captions underneath each one. Ask questions such as "How do you think the sounds were made?" and "What made the sounds different?" Lead the children to understand that moving air makes the sound.

Activity 2: Plan and carry out a changing sound investigation.
(adult help required)
Objective: To understand that sounds are quieter after passing through some materials. To make observations about sounds.
Resources: Woollen scarf, fleece material, cardboard box, plastic box etc
Task: As a group plan the investigation by discussing the headings of the boxes found on the planning sheets. (N.B. The first planning sheet is harder than the second one.) Place all the different materials on the table for the children to look at, touch and hold. They must plan their investigation carefully, thinking about the loudness of the alarm clock and what would make it quieter. All the resources listed are things to put around/ on top of the alarm clock.

Activity 3: Plan and carry out a plucking sound investigation.
(adult help required)
Objective: To understand that sounds can be made in many different ways. To recognise that when they make sounds something moves/ vibrates.
Resources: elastic bands of the same length and thickness, lollipop sticks, various boxes, rulers, wooden blocks, sellotape, blu-tac, split pins, paper clips etc.
Task: Place everything in the middle of the table for the children to choose equipment to make their own 'elastic band guitar' by stretching elastic bands over boxes. Later, as a group, plan an investigation to compare the guitars made by discussing the headings of the boxes found on the planning sheets. (N.B. The first planning sheet is harder than the second one.) The investigation should show even though the same type of elastic bands were used the guitars will make different sounds due to the different designs.

Activity 4: Plan and carry out a 'Sound Source' investigation.
(adult help required)
Objective: To understand that sounds get fainter as they travel away from a source. To measure distances using standard and non-standard measures. To make, record measurements and make comparisons between their results.
Resources: buzzer, door bell or other loud sound source e.g. musical instrument or CD player.
Task: Show the buzzer/ door bell to the group and ask each child to listen to the sound. Ask: Is the sound loud or quiet? Would these sounds be heard from the school hall/ school office? As a group plan the investigation by discussing the headings of the boxes found on the planning sheets. (N.B. The first planning sheet is harder than the second one.) Complete a results chart together as a group.

Plenary
Gather the class together and ask the children to tell a partner two new things they have found out from the investigations. Share these with the class and write them up on the board. Talk about what makes an investigation fair.

Plan and Carry Out a Listening Investigation

Name: _____ Date: _____

My question is... **How can straw whistles make different sounds?**

Equipment List

- straws
- scissors
- sellotape

Method

Find a straw.

Flatten one end.

Cut a point.

Blow over the point.

I will change

I will keep this the same

I will blow gently into each straw in the same way.

I will measure and record

This is how I will make my test fair

I predict that:

Some useful words: longer, shorter, higher, lower, pitch, attach, join, play.

Plan and Carry Out a Listening Investigation

Name: .... Date: ....

My question is...
How can straw whistles make different sounds?

What I will need:

Straws cut like this.

What I will do:

I predict that:

Word Bank

longer, shorter, higher, lower, pitch, attach, join, play.

Plan and Carry Out a Changing Sound Investigation

Name: _____   **Date:** _____

My question is... How can we make the alarm clock make less noise?

Equipment List

- woollen scarf
- fleece material
- cardboard box
- bubble wrap
- plastic box

Method

I will change

I will keep this the same

The object will stay on the table.

I will measure and record

This is how I will make my test fair

I predict that:

Some useful words: wrap, fluffy, cover, inside, muffle, insulate.

Plan and Carry Out a Changing Sound Investigation

Name: Date:

My question is... How can we make the alarm clock make less noise?

What I will need:

What I will do:

I predict that:

Word Bank

wrap, fluffy, cover, inside, muffle, insulate.

Plan and Carry Out a Plucking Sound Investigation

Name: _____   Date: _____

My question is... How can we use elastic bands to make sounds?

Equipment List

Choose from
- cardboard boxes
- ruler
- Sellotape
- Blu-tac
- elastic bands of different sizes
- lollipop sticks
- split pins
- paper clips
- wooden blocks

Method

I will change

I will keep this the same

I will measure and record

Which instrument makes the best sound.

This is how I will make my test fair

I predict that:

Some useful words: stretch, tighten, pluck, pull, loosen, bend, twist, play.

Plan and Carry Out a Plucking Sound Investigation

Name: _____   **Date:** _____

My question is... How can we use elastic bands to make sounds?

What I will need:

What I will do:

I predict that:

Word Bank

stretch, tighten, pluck, pull, loosen, bend, twist, play.

Plan and Carry Out a Sound Source Investigation

Name: _____ **Date:** _____

My question is...
Do sounds get fainter?

Equipment List

Method

I will change

I will keep this the same

The position of the sound source in the room.

I will measure and record

The distance between myself and the source.

This is how I will make my test fair

I predict that:

Some useful words: nearer, further, away, listen, move, stand, stop.

Plan and Carry Out a Sound Source Investigation

Name: _____ Date: _____

My question is...
Do sounds get fainter?

What I will need:

What I will do:

I predict that:

Word Bank

nearer, further, away, listen, move, stand, stop.

Assessment Questions

Name: _____   Date: _____

The teacher will need a selection of instruments used in the activities on the table.

Question	Teacher's Comment
Level 1	
1 Name an instrument you can hit to make a noise.	
2 Name an instrument you can pluck to make a noise.	
3 Name an instrument you can blow to make a noise.	

Question	Teacher's Comment
Level 2	
1 What is the opposite of a loud sound?	
2 What is the opposite of a high sound?	
3 How can you make a drum sound louder?	

Question	Teacher's Comment
Level 3 *A girl plays a drum and you hear it.*	
1 What did the sound travel through to reach your ear?	
2 What happens to the sound of the drum being played as you walk further away from it?	
3 What is the source of the sound?	
4 Without moving away, how could this sound be made quieter?	

Knowledge of Sound and Hearing Record of Attainment Class: _____ Date: _____				Level 1 Communicate observations of changes in sound that result from actions. Recognise that sound comes from a variety of sources and name some of these.	Level 2 Know about a range of physical phenomena and recognise and describe similarities and differences associated with them. Compare the loudness or pitch of sounds.	Level 3 Use their knowledge and understanding of physical phenomena to link cause and effect in simple explanations and begin to make simple generalisations about physical phenomena.

Forces and Motion

Main Objective:
To understand that pushing or pulling things can make objects start or stop moving, slow down or speed up.

Talk about:
Using a selection of objects at the front of the room, ask the children to show how some things move, e.g. toy cars, a doll's pram, a football, small shopping trolley etc. Encourage the children to talk about what happens to each object using the words **'push'** and **'pull'**. Write down the two words on large pieces of card and ask two children to hold these up at the front of the room. Each time you point to one of the cards all the children need to show a mime. For example they could show pushing a trolley or pulling a rope. Carry out this activity and choose different children each time to explain what action they were miming. See if other children can guess what they were doing. Introduce the term 'a force' and explain that a **pull is a 'force'** and a **push is a 'force'**.

Activity 1: Push or Pull?
Objective: To observe and describe different ways of moving.
Resources: Play dough, play dough boards, moulding tools and a cloth to wipe hands
Task: Follow the directions on Activity Sheet 1 to make different play dough shapes. The children will draw each shape they have made and then write yes or no in each column to show how they have made it. They can talk about their ideas and use the same shapes as other children in their group if they wish. After the activity they can make more shapes of their own.

Activity 2: Slowing things down
(adult help required)
Objective: To describe how things can slow down. To make suggestions about how objects can be made to move and to find out whether they were right.
Resources: toy car and small wooden ramp, tennis ball and other resources, which move easily, to give the children further ideas.
Task: Each group member will try out the toy car and the ball and then talk about how they were slowed down. Each time they will record their ideas on Activity Sheet 2. The children should be encouraged to invent different ways of slowing the objects down. Ask questions such as "How did you slow the toy car down? Are there any other ways of doing this? Which method worked the best?" etc. The blank boxes are for the children to think of their own ideas for everyday classroom objects to slow down.

Activity 3: Speeding things up
(adult help required)
Objective: To describe how things can speed up. To make suggestions about how objects can be made to move and to find out whether they were right.
Resources: Outdoor equipment including scooter, tennis ball, Frisbee, roller blades/ boots, football etc.
Task: The children will take turns to use some of the objects and show the rest of the group how they move and then how they speed up. Talk about what they did and ask questions such as "How did they manage to speed up?' How did they know they were going faster?" The children could first share their ideas with the group then record their ideas on Activity Sheet 3.

Activity 4: Push or Pull? You Decide!
Objective: To observe and describe different ways of moving. To recognise that pushing or pulling objects can make them stop or start moving.
Resources: Activity sheet 4
Task: Follow the instructions on the sheet to circle the push/pull answers underneath each picture. When individuals have finished they can make their own push/pull pictures for the group to guess.

Plenary
Ask the children to talk to their partner about three things they have found out about 'pushes' and 'pulls' and then share these with the class. Write some of these on the board to refer to later. Give each pair a small ball of play dough. Use cards with the words: twist, stretch, turn, bend, push, pull, press, flatten and hold up one at a time. They must follow the instruction on the card using the play dough ball. Finally ask the children to make a dough shape with their partner and then decide whether they used a push, a pull or both forces in the construction.

Push or Pull?

Name: ---------------------------------- **Date:** ----------------------------------

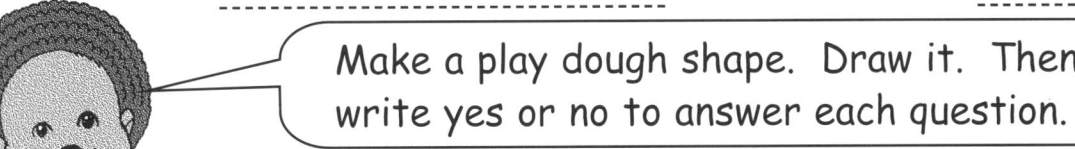

Make a play dough shape. Draw it. Then write yes or no to answer each question.

Draw your shapes below.	Did You....				
	Stretch it? (Pull)	Twist it? (Pull)	Squash it? (Push)	Bend it? (Pull)	Roll it? (Push)

Now make some different shapes from play dough.

Slowing Things Down

Name: _____   **Date:** _____

Make these things move and then decide 'How to slow them down.'

toy car

I slowed this down by...

_____

_____

tennis ball

I slowed this down by...

_____

_____

Now make some other classroom objects move.
Draw them below and write 'How to slow them down.'

I slowed this down by...

_____

_____

I slowed this down by...

_____

_____

Speeding Things Up

Name: Date:

How would you make these things speed up?
Draw and write your ideas.

scooter

I would speed this up by...

_____

football

I would speed this up by...

_____

frisbee

I would speed this up by...

_____

roller
skates

I would speed this up by...

_____

tennis ball

I would speed this up by...

_____

Think of other things you can speed up.
Draw them on the back of this sheet.

Push or Pull?-You Decide

Name: _____ **Date:** _____

Look at the pictures and then circle each correct answer. Try some out.

1
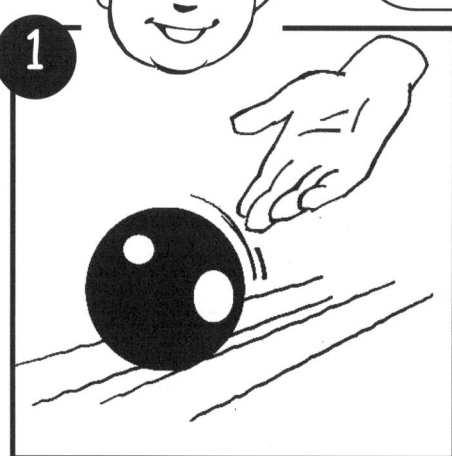
Push or **Pull?**

2
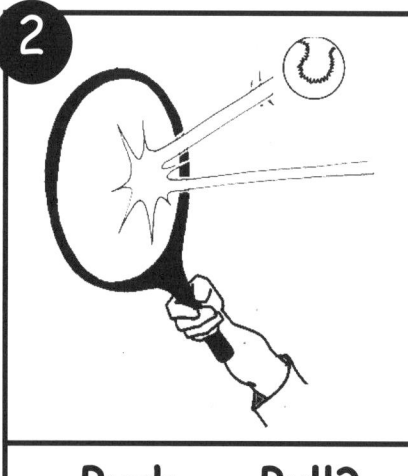
Push or **Pull?**

3

Push or **Pull?**

4

Push or **Pull?**

5

Push or **Pull?**

6

Push or **Pull?**

7

Push or **Pull?**

8

Push or **Pull?**

9

Push or **Pull?**

Draw some pictures of your own. Is it a pull? Is it a push? Ask your group to decide.

Main Objective:
To understand that forces can make objects move and that gravity is an invisible force.

Talk about:
Use a selection of toy windmills, water wheels and sand wheels. Show the children how these work at the front of the class.

Ask some children to try to explain what makes these objects move. Encourage them to use the words push, pull, twist, turn etc. Then make a list on the board of objects they know about at home and at school that twiste e.g. door knobs, pepper mills, wind up toys etc.

Activity 1: Moving Cars
(adult help required)
Objective: To identify similarities and differences between the movement of objects. To make measurements of distance using standard and non-standard measures. To decide whether the comparison was fair.

Resources: Toy cars, small wooden ramp, blocks for the ramp to stand on, measuring equipment.

Task: Use Activity Sheet 1 to discuss ideas about the toy car and ramp test. Talk with the children about the following ideas, "How will the car move down the ramp? How can we make it travel further each time? What do you need to keep the same to make it a fair test? What will we need to measure? How will we record our results each time? Why do the cars travel further?" After each attempt they will draw and write their results on the activity sheet. Each distance will need to be measured accurately and recorded. After the test ask the children the questions on the bottom of the sheet.

Activity 2: Air Powered Rockets
(adult help required)
Objective: To predict what will happen. To say whether the prediction was correct and to try to explain the results. To ask questions about what is causing movement and to identify the cause of motion.

Resources: To make the rocket(s): card or paper rolled into a tube, wings/ nose attached made out of card or paper. See Activity Sheet 2 for drawing of the rocket launch pad using large empty plastic pop bottle, strong tape, piece of wood, plastic pipe from DIY store. (This may be prepared in advance.)

Task: Demonstrate how a cardboard tube rocket can be launched using compressed air pushed out of the plastic bottle as you stamp on it. Talk about how the air is pushed out of the bottle and into the pipe to push the rocket into the air. Explain how an invisible force called 'gravity' pulls the rocket back down to the ground when it falls. Let the children use card and paper to make their own rockets to test on the rocket launcher. Record what they did on Activity Sheet 2. Finally talk about which rocket worked best and possible reasons for this.

Activity 3: What if...? Game
Objective: To recognise hazards and risks to themselves from moving objects. To describe examples where pushes and pulls alter movement.

Resources: Activity Sheet 3 copied onto card and cut out.

Task: Place the picture cards face down on the table. The children should take turns to turn over a card and explain what would happen if the drawing on the card came true. They should share their ideas with the group after which other children will award them a score between 1 and 5. Each child keeps their own score and the card they have chosen. At the end of the game the winner is the one with the most points. Next they can make up and draw their own 'What if...?' cards and play the game again.

Activity 4: Play the True/ False Forces Game
Objective: To make suggestions about the speed objects can be made to move and to find out whether they were right.

Resources: Several pieces of A4 paper, football, marble, feather, pencil, ruler and book, soft surface for the objects to land on, green and red coloured pencils/ crayons or felt tips. Large sheet of paper.

Task: Using the selection of objects provided and Activity Sheet 4, the children will take turns to try out each true/ false statement. If the statement is true then colour 'TRUE' in green. If the statement is false they colour 'FALSE' in red. At the end they should talk to the group in turn to say what happened. The group should then draw some of their ideas on a large piece of paper with arrows showing the direction of fall of the objects. This will be used to share with the class in the plenary.

Plenary
Use the large sheets of paper completed during Activity 4. Talk about what the children have discovered during their activities. Sing 'Here we go round the Mulberry bush' together and ask the children about the forces involved in each verse. Carry out the actions as a class.

Moving Cars

Name: _____ **Date:** _____

How far can you make a toy car go?
Use a ramp and blocks to help you.

 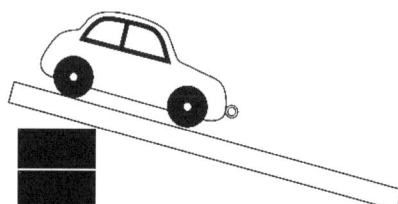

?   ?

| **Attempt 1** | Prediction: |
| | Distance Measured: |

| **Attempt 2** | Prediction: |
| | Distance Measured: |

| **Attempt 3** | Prediction: |
| | Distance Measured: |

| **Attempt 4** | Prediction: |
| | Distance Measured: |

What did you change? What did you leave the same? Did you predict correctly? Was your test fair? Why did the car move?

Air Powered Rockets

Name: _____   **Date:** _____

You will need a rocket launcher made from a plastic bottle like this.

plastic pipe   sticky tape   plastic bottle

Make some model rockets from cardboard tubes. Cover the top and decorate.

1	2	3
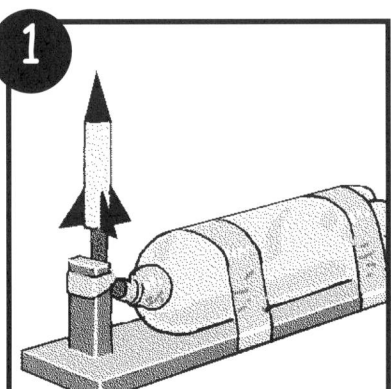	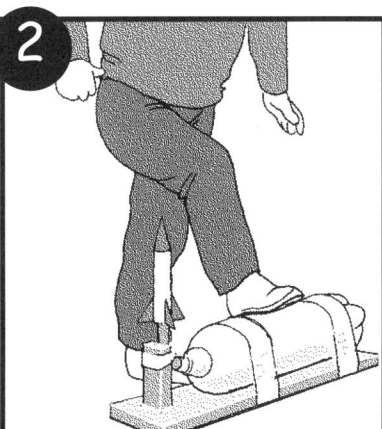	
Place the rocket on the launcher.	Stamp hard on the bottle.	What happens? Why?

Draw and write what happened.

_____

_____

_____

_____

Talk to your group about which rocket worked the best. Can you improve on this?

What if..?
Questions Game

What if...

prams could
only be pulled?

What if...

cars had to push caravans?

What if...

front doors
pushed
outwards?

What if...

lawnmowers
were
pulled?

What if...

supermarket
trolleys had
to be pulled?

Play the True/False Forces Game

Name:

Date:

Try out these statements. Colour the word  or **False** each time.

The flat piece of paper will fall to the floor before the screwed up ball.	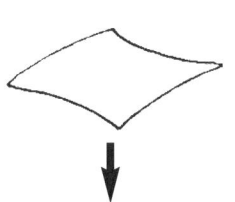	**True** / **False**
The folded piece of paper will fall to the floor before the flat piece.	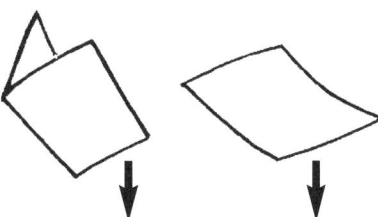	**True** / **False**
The paper balls will land on the floor at the same time.		**True** / **False**
The football and the marble will land on the floor at the same time.		**True** / **False**
The feather will fall to the floor before the pencil.	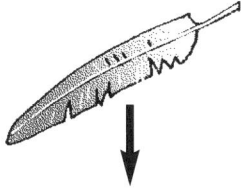	**True** / **False**
The ruler will fall to the floor quicker than the book.	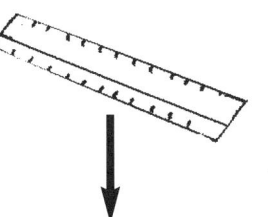	**True** / **False**

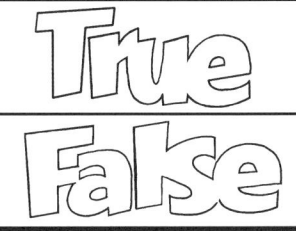

Talk to your group about what happened. Draw a picture showing 'Gravity' pulling things down.

Main Objective:
To make predictions, observations, simple comparisons and explain these.

Talk about:
Hold up some of the resources from the different investigation tables. Ask the children to think about what they might be used for, for example hold up a toy car and a piece of floor covering. Ask "How could we use these objects in a fair test?" Then hold up the marble and a ramp and ask "What can we try to find out today?" Encourage the children to think about making sensible predictions. Give some examples of silly predictions about the investigations e.g. "I predict that the toy car will travel to another classroom! I predict that the marble will roll really far if I put a brick in front of it! I predict the balloon will pop!"

Activity 1: Plan and carry out a moving object investigation.
(adult help required)
Objective: To decide the best way to make a marble roll as far as possible. To measure distances carefully in appropriate units.
Resources: Marble, wooden ramp, wooden blocks to go under the ramp.
Task: As a group plan the investigation by discussing the headings of the boxes found on the planning sheets. (N.B. The first planning sheet is harder than the second one.) The children should devise ideas for the test making sure that they use the same marble each time but change one other factor such as the height of the ramp. They will need to think about where the starting point for the roll is going to be and how they will make sure that it is always the same place by making a mark or some other method. The children will take turns to measure each marble roll and record the results in a way decided on by the whole group. If each group records their results in a slightly different way then this gives a good basis for discussion during the plenary.

Activity 2: Plan and carry out a friction investigation,
(adult help required)
Objective: To know that the rougher the surface, the greater the friction. To decide what to do and what measurements to make.
Resources: A toy car, a fixed wooden ramp leading to different surfaces e.g. thin carpet, thick carpet, corrugated cardboard, bubble wrap, sandpaper, lino etc. Rulers, tape measures to measure distance travelled.
Task: As a group plan the investigation by discussing the headings of the boxes found on the planning sheets. (N.B. The first planning sheet is harder than the second one.) The children should decide which surfaces to test from the variety of materials provided. They will then have to decide on the starting point for

each car and how to measure the distance they will travel. The starting point must always be the same. Ask questions such as "What makes the car move? What might make the car slow down or stop? Why should we always start from the same starting point?" The children should record their results on a chart showing the distance travelled by the toy car and the type of surface used. Encourage the children to use the word 'friction' when talking about the resistance to movement offered by the different surfaces.

Activity 3: Plan and carry out an air powered balloon investigion.
(adult help required)
Objective: To make comparisons between the movement of different objects. To use results to make comparisons and to evaluate whether the test was fair. To use results in a table to draw a block graph.
Resources: Balloons of different shapes and sizes, fine string, straws, sticky tape, tape measure.
Task: As a group plan the investigation by discussing the headings of the boxes found on the planning sheets. (N.B. The first planning sheet is harder than the second one.) The children should look at each balloon before it is pumped with air and make predictions about which one they think will travel furthest along the stretched string. Ask questions such as "How do you think the balloon will move? Why does it move so quickly?" etc. The children will watch each balloon and record the distance travelled. The results can be presented on a block graph.

Activity 4: Plan and carry out a floating object investigation.
(adult help required)
Objective: To understand that water can push up objects and this is called 'Upthrust'.
Resources: plastic tubs, plastic ruler, toy car, marble, weights, empty plastic bottle, various other objects if possible including a conker, a plastic duck, a stone etc.
Task: Introduce the term 'Upthrust'. As a group plan the investigation by discussing the headings of the boxes found on the planning sheets. (N.B. The first planning sheet is harder than the second one.) The children should be expected to make sensible predictions before testing the various objects in the tub of water. Ask questions such as "What is pulling the object down? What is pushing the object up?" etc. Children should record their observations.

Plenary
Gather the class together and ask the children to tell a partner new things they have found out from the investigations. Ask individual pupils to share these with the rest of the class. Talk about which surfaces slowed the toy car down best and which ramp made the marble go furthest. Talk about what made the ballon move and what held up the objects in the water.

Plan and Carry Out a Moving Object Investigation

Name: _____   Date: _____

My question is...
What makes a marble roll further?

Equipment List

Method

I will change

I will keep this the same

The type of marble used. The starting point for the roll.

I will measure and record

The distance the marble travels.

This is how I will make my test fair

I predict that:

Some useful words: ramp, push, change, measure, ruler, tape measure, higher, lower.

Plan and Carry Out a Moving Object Investigation

Name: _____   Date: _____

My question is...
What makes a marble roll further?

What I will need:

What I will do:

I predict that:

Word Bank
ramp, push, change, measure, ruler, tape measure, higher, lower.

Plan and Carry Out a Friction Investigation

Name: _____ **Date:** _____

My question is... Which surface is best for a toy car to travel on?

Equipment List

Method

I will change

The surface used.

I will keep this the same

The ramp height and angle.
The starting point of the car.

I will measure and record

This is how I will make my test fair

I predict that:

Some useful words: stopwatch, timer, count, fast, slow, quick.

Plan and Carry Out a Friction Investigation

Name: _____ **Date:** _____

My question is... Which surface is best for a toy car to travel on?

What I will need:

What I will do:

I predict that:

Word Bank

stopwatch, timer, count, fast, slow, quick.

Plan and Carry Out an Air Powered Balloon Investigation

Name: _____   Date: _____

My question is...
Which balloons travel the furthest along the string?

Equipment List

Method

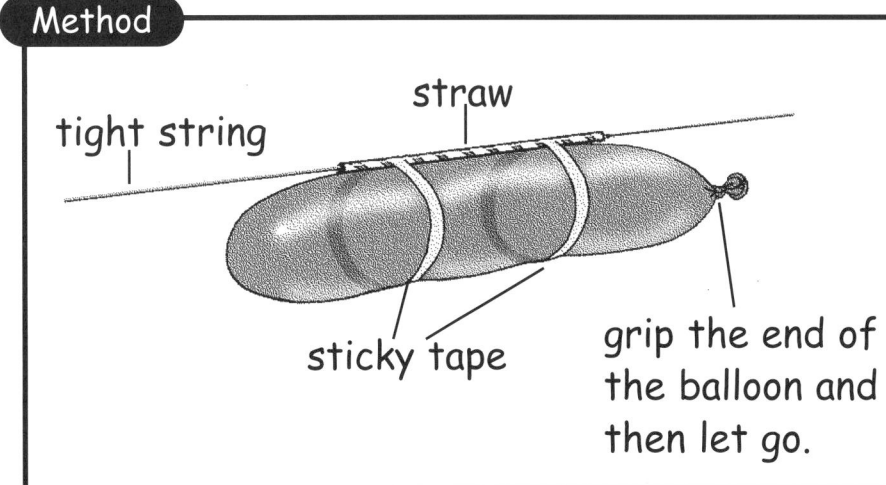

tight string

straw

sticky tape

grip the end of the balloon and then let go.

I will change

The type of balloon each time.

I will keep this the same

I will measure and record

This is how I will make my test fair

I predict that:

Some useful words: straw, wire, attach, release, tape.

Plan and Carry Out an Air Powered Balloon Investigation

Name:

Date:

My question is... Which balloons travel the furthest along the string?

What I will need:

tight string

straw

sticky tape

grip the end of the balloon and then let go.

What I will do:

I predict that:

Word Bank

straw, wire, attach, release, tape.

Plan and Carry Out a Floating Object Investigation

Name: _____ **Date:** _____

My question is...
Which objects float and why?

Equipment List

- plastic tubs
- marble
- weights etc.

Method

I will change

The objects will be different each time.

I will keep this the same

I will measure and record

This is how I will make my test fair

I predict that:

Some useful words:
pull, push, water, weight, object, sink, heavy, gravity

Plan and Carry Out a Floating Object Investigation

Name: ....   **Date:** ....

My question is...
Which objects float and why?

What I will need:

What I will do:

I predict that:

Word Bank

pull, push, water, weight, object, sink, heavy, gravity

Assessment Questions

Name: _____ Date: _____

The teacher should place a selection of objects/equipment used in the activities on the table for the child to work with.

Question	Teacher's Comment
Level 1	
1 What is a force?	
2 Name an object you could move with a push.	
3 Name an object you could move with a pull.	

Question	Teacher's Comment
Level 2	
1 What size of kick makes a fooball move quickly - big or small?	
2 What size of kick makes a fooball move slowly - big or small?	
3 How can you make a slowly rolling football change direction?	

Question	Teacher's Comment
Level 3	
1 Which is easiest to push across a smooth table - a brick or a toy car?	
2 Why do you think your above answer is correct?	
3 Name a machine that can pull things.	
4 Name a force in nature that can push you along.	

Knowledge of Forces

Record of Attainment

Class: _____

Date: _____

	Level 1	Level 2	Level 3
	Communicate observations of changes in movement that result from actions e.g. pushing and pulling objects.	Compare the movement of different objects in terms of speed or direction.	Link cause and effect in simple explanations e.g. the direction or speed of movement of an object changing because of a push or pull.